ERIC HEIDEN

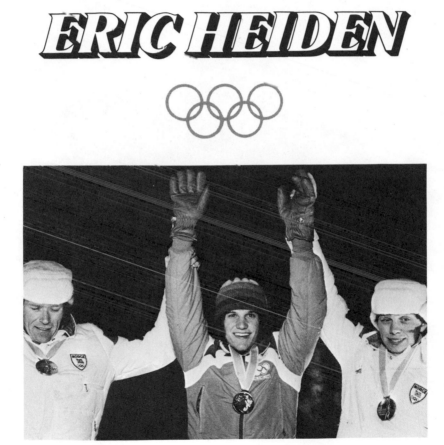

ERIC HEIDEN
Winner in Gold

Nathan Aaseng

Lerner Publications Company ■ Minneapolis

Not Ap

ACKNOWLEDGMENTS: The photographs are reproduced through the courtesy of: pp. 1, 2, 6, 9, 11, 13, 14, 15, 16, 17, 27, 29, 30, 33, 34, 36, 37, 38, 40, 41, 42, 43, 45, 46, 48, 49, 50, 51, 53, 55, Wide World Photos, Inc.; pp. 19, 20, 21, 22, 23, 25, 54, John E. Biever.

Cover photograph by Heinz Kluetmeier, *Sports Illustrated* © 1980 Time, Inc.

To the Reverend E. E. Olson

LIBRARY OF CONGRESS CATALOGING IN PUBLICATION DATA

Aaseng, Nathan.
    Eric Heiden: Winner in gold.

    (The achievers)
    SUMMARY: Presents the skating career of Eric Heiden. the American speedskater who won five gold medals at the 1980 Olympics.

    1. Heiden, Eric—Juvenile literature.   2. Skaters—United States—Biography—Juvenile literature.   3. Speed skating—Juvenile literature.   4. Olympic Games (Winter) Lake Placid. N.Y., 1980—Juvenile literature. [1. Heiden, Eric. 2. Ice skaters. 3. Speed skating.   4. Olympic Games (Winter) Lake Placid. N.Y., 1980] I. Title.   II. Series: Achievers.

GV850.H37Aa62   1980   796.91′092′4 [B] [92]   80-16982
ISBN 0-8225-0481-2   (lib. bdg.)

Manufactured in the United States of America. Published simultaneously in Canada by J. M. Dent & Sons (Canada) Ltd., Don Mills, Ontario.

International Standard Book Number: 0-8225-0481-2
Library of Congress Catalog Card Number: 80-16982

1 2 3   4 5 6 7 8 9 10 85 84 83 82 81 80

ERIC HEIDEN

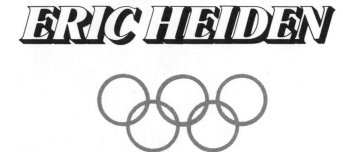

"Do you think you will win five gold medals?"

Eric Heiden had heard this question all week long. People were expecting him to win five speedskating races in the 1980 Winter Olympics. The record holder for gold medals was U.S. swimmer Mark Spitz. In 1972 Spitz had won seven gold medals, but three of them were team medals. No one had ever won five individual gold medals in an Olympics. It was a lot to ask of a 21 year old—it was a lot to ask of anyone!

Eric had already won one gold medal. To win four more gold medals, he would have to beat several world record holders at their best events. He would have to win every race from the short sprints to the longest distance. So much pressure and attention would have turned most athletes into nervous wrecks. But at this moment on Saturday, February 16, Eric Heiden was free from all questions and microphones.

5

Tom Erik Oxholm was one of Heiden's strongest competitors in the 5,000-meter race.

It was time for Heiden to think about his second race, the 5,000-meter race, which was already underway. A young man named Tom Erik Oxholm of Norway had given him plenty to think about. Only a short time ago, Oxholm had skated the 2.1-mile distance in just over 7 minutes, 5 seconds. That was more than 16 seconds faster than the old Olympic record!

Olympic speedskaters race in pairs around a 400-meter ice rink. When all the contestants have had a chance to race, medals are awarded to those with the fastest times. So Heiden had more to worry about than just beating the man who would skate next to him in his race. He had to beat Oxholm's time.

Eric was doing a lot of thinking, as he always does before a big race. In his mind, he was going over all the things he had to do to skate a perfect race. In a long race such as this 5,000-meter race, he wanted to keep an even pace. He knew it was important to spread his energy over the whole race so that his last bit of strength would send him to the finish line. Of course it was going to hurt. His lungs would beg for air, and his muscles would feel as heavy as if they were made of cement. Eric thought about what he would do when his body started hurting. His gold medal depended on how hard he could push himself *after* he was tired.

The stands at the rink in Lake Placid, New York, were packed with American fans. The crowd was watching Heiden closely as he moved over to the starting line. The man who looked like a comic book superhero in his bright gold stretch suit was about to try for his second gold medal.

The gun went off. The crowd cheered wildly. Heiden dashed across the ice with quick, short strides until he built up speed. Soon he switched to long, smooth strokes, gliding easily around the curves.

The large scoreboard clock showed the spectators that Heiden was not keeping up with Oxholm's time. Oxholm had skated a magnificent race, and at the halfway point, Eric's time was a full two seconds slower than Oxholm's. Eric's mother, Nancy Heiden, could not bear to watch the clock anymore. She was afraid Eric had lost too much ground to win the race.

Eric was starting to feel the tiredness and pain. He knew the aches would be getting worse with each lap. This was the time he had been preparing for. In the next three minutes, Eric would find out if he was ready to meet the challenge of another gold medal.

When Eric's parents first gave him a pair of ice skates, they were not thinking about Olympic medals and howling crowds. Eric's father was a surgeon who knew how important it was to exercise. A cold winter day was no excuse for a Heiden to sit indoors.

Eric received his first pair of skates when he was two years old.
At age five (*above*) he was photographed with E. H. Carpenter,
a well-known Madison skater and coach.

The Heiden home in Madison, Wisconsin, was close to lakes that easily froze in Wisconsin's frigid winters. Much of Eric's early skating was done on these lakes. The whole family, including Eric's younger sister, Beth, often spent weekends touring the beautiful bays and inlets on skates.

When Eric and Beth were in grade school, they took figure skating lessons at the Madison Skating Club. The Heidens were hardly ideal students! They would race each other from one end of the rink to the other, causing trouble and disrupting the other students. Finally they were asked to quit the class.

Eric tried playing hockey in the peewee leagues for a while, but he did not get really serious about skating until junior high. That was when he met Dianne Holum. Holum had skated in the 1968 and 1972 Olympics. She was a speedskater who owned four Olympic medals, including a gold from the 1972 Olympics. Everything Holum said about the life of racing sounded great to Eric, and he began to put all his energy into speedskating.

Eric's new enthusiasm for skating was shared by his sister, Beth. Eric and Beth were now racing around the rink with a real purpose in mind. Dianne Holum was excited by what she saw. What really impressed her was their hard work and enthusiasm.

Dianne Holum (*left*) won a gold medal in the 1,500-meter race at the 1972 Olympics in Sapporo, Japan.

She knew they could be good, and she spent most of the next eight years coaching them.

In the United States, speedskating can be a very lonely sport. There are no more than a couple hundred active racers in the country. Even at some of the more important meets there are more timers and race judges at the rink than spectators. Worse yet, until the Lake Placid rink was finished in 1978, the only Olympic-size rink in the United Sates was in West Allis, Wisconsin.

Fortunately for Eric and Beth, the West Allis rink was in their home state, but they still had to travel 70 miles to get there. And once there, they had to pay for the use of the ice. Even if it was bitterly cold, the Heidens stayed for hours to make the trip worthwhile. They spent much of their time practicing turns. Turning is one of the most important parts of speedskating. Skaters cannot use the same sweeping strides on curves that they use on straightaways. If they did, they would go flying off the track.

Frequently it seems to skaters as though their hard work doesn't do much good. Many skaters lose interest in the sport after a few years. But the Heidens never gave up. They hoped that sooner or later they would start improving their times in races. In the meantime, they enjoyed the challenge of skating. They liked the feeling of trying to beat their best times.

Training never seemed boring to Eric and Beth because it changed when the seasons changed. Believe it or not, ice skaters spend more time training off the ice than they do on it. When the weather is warm, skaters do exercises that include running and bicycling. By the time those exercises start to get dull, the cold air is back, and they lace up their skates for their winter training.

Beth Heiden was the youngest member of the 1976 United States Olympic team.

Both Eric and Beth made the United States Olympic speedskating team in 1976. Though Eric was only 17, and Beth 16, they held their own against the older European skaters. Eric finished 7th in the 1,500-meter race and 19th in the 5,000 meter. Beth took 11th place in the women's 3,000 meter. But their performances in the 1976 Olympics in Montreal were not enough to cause American sports fans to take a second look at them.

In 1977 Eric won three international speedskating titles in three weeks, including the World Sprint Speedskating Championship (*above*).

The following year Eric skated in the World Speedskating Championships. He hoped that his hard training would bring him a second or two closer to the top skaters. But when he started racing, something

14

Skating victories brought fame to both Eric and Beth in 1977. While Eric won the Men's World Junior Speedskating, the Men's World Speedskating, and the Men's World Sprint Speedskating Championships, Beth placed second, fourth, and seventh, respectively, in the women's events.

seemed strange. All of a sudden Eric was beating everyone! Heiden could not figure it out, and neither could his opponents. One day Eric was a fairly good skater, and the next day he was unbeatable. It was as though he had stumbled upon a magic formula that turned him into a champion. He won the overall championship that year. It was the first time an American had earned the title since 1891!

15

Both Eric and Beth won the World Junior Speedskating Championships in 1978. As he had done in 1977, Eric also won the World Speedskating and the World Sprint Speedskating Championships.

But the *only* magic formula Eric had used was hard work. When he saw how much his workouts were helping him, it made him want to practice even more. Proving that the 1977 performance was more than just an amazing string of luck, Eric also won the World Championships in 1978 and 1979. Beth matched his performance in 1979. Although she stood just 5 feet, 1 inch, and weighed only 100 pounds, she won every one of the four events in the women's competition.

Beth Heiden (*center*) with the second- and third-place winners at the 1979 World Speedskating Championships. Beth won all four women's events—the 500-, the 1,000-, the 1,500-, and the 3,000-meter races.

The Heidens became heroes in Europe after so many successful World Championships. While in Europe for the championships, they visited such places as Norway and the Netherlands, where skating is the national sport. In these countries, they were mobbed like rock stars. Eric and Beth could hardly step outside a hotel without being recognized.

Eric's daredevil nature also brought him plenty of attention. During one stay in Italy, Eric decided he would like to try his luck at a nearby bobsled run. Little did he know the run crossed the busy section of town and was not to be used except at certain times of the day. Heiden zoomed down the course and missed a turn near the bottom. The next thing he knew, he was bobsledding into heavy traffic on one of the town's busier streets. Fortunately no one was hurt.

Another time Eric caused quite a fuss when a picture of him appeared in Norwegian newspapers. A photographer had caught Eric and his buddies celebrating a win by skating a victory lap in their underwear!

When Eric and Beth returned to the United States, after the 1979 World Championships they found they were back to being ordinary people. They could still spend a whole day traveling around their home town of Madison and never be noticed. That was just fine with them. Both Heidens agreed that it was much more peaceful being "unknowns." Besides, they enjoyed being able to do whatever they liked without being watched all the time. People in the United States paid very little attention to Eric and Beth as they prepared for the 1980 Olympics.

Timed by Coach Dianne Holum (*left*), Eric and other prospective Olympic speedskaters train near the Heiden home in Madison, Wisconsin.

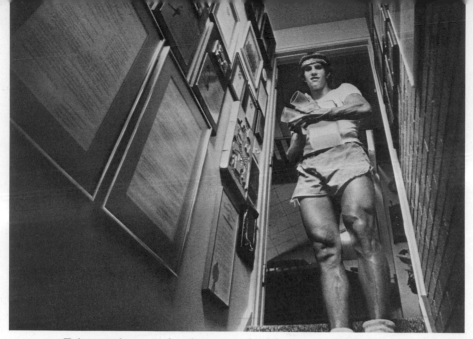

Eric works out in the gym in his home with Dianne Holum (*right*). Taking a break, he walks through a hallway filled with skating plaques.

The European skaters, however, had all eyes on Eric. They were still trying to learn the secret of his unusual success. Again, they were disappointed by the reports of his training schedule. He didn't do anything they weren't doing. As before, Eric's only magic formula was hard work. He attacked his exercises like a wild cat going after its dinner. He ran long distances and sprinted shorter ones in quick succession. Wearing an inner tube filled with birdshot, he did power bends and squats to build up skating muscles.

Every day during practice Eric ran 10 miles and bicycled up to 100 miles. He also skated many laps around the ice rink in West Allis, Wisconsin.

Thanks to a clever Russian invention, Eric could also skate outdoors in the summer. He wore summer skates that had three narrow wheels in a line down the center of the skate. It felt very much like skating on ice. Biking, jumping, and running up and down steep hills also filled his time.

During one workout in the Rocky Mountains, Eric and his teammates were stopped by a squad car. The policemen thought the boys were hitchhiking, which was against the law. The skaters ended up by getting a free ride back down to the 1980 Olympic training camp before it was all straightened out. This could never have happened in Europe where Eric would have been recognized instantly.

As the winter months drew near, the Heidens' days as unknown American sports stars were ending. Since the Olympics were being held in the United States at Lake Placid, New York, Americans were on the lookout for possible heroes. Many people would be able to go to the Olympics and actually *see* someone from their own country do well. When reporters were told Eric was so good he had a chance to win five gold medals, they decided to watch him closely. They also kept their eyes on Beth, and they expected her to win at least two gold medals.

Beth works out on an electric tension device while Dianne times her.

When Eric and Beth arrived at Lake Placid, New York, for the Olympics, the questions and pictures and telephone calls started. They made a point of staying away from all phones. Their parents hired Arthur Kaminsky, a lawyer from New York, to handle some of the reporters. Kaminsky's job of keeping people away from Eric and Beth made him a most unpopular man. Still the Heidens could not go anywhere near the Olympic village without people making a big deal over them.

Somehow Eric stayed calm through it all. People around him wondered if Eric realized how important the Olympics were. He seemed too peaceful and easygoing to be a competitor. He actually seemed bored by the whole fuss.

But Beth had a much rougher time. Although a great skater, Beth was not the overpowering athlete that Eric was. Yet most people seemed to be expecting as much from her as they did from Eric. This pressure, combined with an ankle injury, was going to make Beth's 1980 Olympic performance a disappointment for many.

United States athletes participate in the opening ceremonies
at the 1980 Olympic games in Lake Placid, New York.

Eric refused to listen to those who predicted five gold medals for him. He said he would be happy to come home with just one. One of Eric's toughest tests would come in the first race, the 500-meter event. If Eric had a weakness, it was in these very short races.

The 500-meter race took place on Friday, February 15. It was the shortest sprint of all. The world record holder in the event, Russia's Evgeni Kulikov, was ready to put Eric to the test. The names of the top 12 skaters in the event were thrown into a cup, and the starting positions for the race were then chosen by draw. As luck would have it, Heiden found he would be skating with Kulikov.

As Heiden and Kulikov moved to the starting line, all eyes seemed to be on Heiden. For most Americans, this was their first look at the man sports fans were starting to talk about. Heiden stands 6 feet, 1 inch, and weighs 185 pounds. Many must have wondered if their televisions were broken because Eric's thighs looked distorted. They seemed far too big to be real! In fact each of his thighs is only three inches smaller than his waist.

Heiden, in his gold suit, and Kulikov, dressed in red, took their starting positions. Both were a little nervous, and they jumped the gun. Back to the

In his first race, the 500-meter event, Eric (*left*) was paired with the world record holder, Evgeni Kulikov.

starting line they went. This time the race started cleanly. Kulikov sped to a narrow lead after the first 100 meters. But he was going so fast he was not in control of himself as he went into the first turn. Slipping slightly, he lost his lead.

Eric swept through the turn without a problem. With their arms whipping from side to side high over their heads, the two men stayed within inches of each other down the backstretch. But Eric shot out of the last turn and stormed to the finish line

29

Heiden moved ahead of Kulikov to win the 500-meter race and to set a new world record.

just ahead of his opponent. Heiden's time of 38.03 seconds was an Olympic record! Kulikov, not far behind at 38.37, had also broken his old Olympic record of 39.17 seconds.

Then all the other pairs of speedskaters had their

chance to try to beat Heiden's mark. But no one came close. Eric had his first gold medal and Kulikov took the silver. As usual Eric's comment was, "I did my best." This is usually what unsuccessful racers say after a contest but Eric says it after some of his most impressive races.

Eric's thrilling first-race match with Kulikov attracted a large television audience who could hardly wait for Heiden's next race. "One down, four to go," he was told. Heiden just shrugged.

Race number two was held the next day. It was the 5,000 meter. Eric did not panic when he found himself far behind the pace of Norway's Oxholm. At one point, his time was about four seconds slower than Oxholm's. Eric kept control over his body. Like a windup skating machine, he traveled each lap in the same amount of time. With his arms and legs pumping in perfect rhythm, he drew closer and closer to Oxholm's pace. By 3,800 meters he was even with the Norwegian's time.

Eric drove his aching muscles on. Same steady pace. Same long stride. He kept his back low and straight. When he crossed the finish line, the scoreboard clock showed 7:02.29 seconds. He had outlasted Oxholm and beaten him by three seconds!

But the suspense was not over yet. Still to come was the race of the 5,000 meter world record holder, Kai Arne Stenshjemmet, Oxholm's Norwegian teammate. As Stenshjemmet cruised his laps, the American crowd grew fidgety. Like his teammate, Stenshjemmet started strongly. But, unlike his teammate, he showed no signs of slowing down. With only two laps to go, he clung stubbornly to Heiden's pace. The crowd watched the clock as nervously as someone who is late for class.

As Stenshjemmet rounded the last corner, it was obvious he was going to come very close. He crossed the finish line in a time of 7:03.28. The crowd could start breathing again—Eric had won the 5,000-meter event by less than one second. But he had broken his second Olympic record by over 20 seconds! Fortunately for Eric, he was not around to sweat out the end of his rival's race. Instead he was calmly sitting in the clubhouse. Two gold medals, three to go.

Eric on the winners' stand with silver medalist Kai Arne Stenshjemmet (*left*) and Tom Erik Oxholm, the third-place finisher, after the 5,000-meter race

Heiden races against Gaetan Boucher in the 1,000-meter event.

The 1,000-meter race was held three days later on Tuesday, February 19. The 1,000-meter race is a long sprint, and Eric knew he could count on his fine physical condition to help him. Heiden's skating opponent was Canadian Gaetan Boucher. As usual, Eric slowly began to build up a lead over his opponent.

The tough races in the first two events had taken

away some of Eric's strength. His breath came in gasps. The frosty winter air made his throat feel as if it was burning. Every one of his muscles seemed to have some complaint, especially those in his left leg. This is the inside leg on all the turns in speed-skating, and it takes extra punishment. It must hold most of the skater's weight as he or she strains to keep from going too wide on the curves.

Eric fought off these aches and finished one and a half seconds ahead of Boucher. His time of 1:15.18 was another Olympic record, his third in three races. While trying to regain his breath, Heiden wondered what his American teammate Peter Mueller would do. Mueller had won the gold medal in this event in the 1976 Olympics. But even though he skated faster than he had in 1976, Mueller did not break into the top three. With a time of 1:17.11, he placed fifth.

Eric seemed to bring out the best in his opponents as well in himself. Though he was beaten by Heiden, Boucher wound up with the silver medal. It was the second time Eric's partner had taken second place.

Even after his easy victory, Heiden would not predict that he would win five gold medals. So many races in such a short time is very hard on a body, and Eric was starting to feel tired.

In the 3,000-meter race, Beth Heiden placed third and Bjoers Eva Jensen (*center*) of Norway won the gold medal.

On the following day, Wednesday, February 20, it was Beth's turn to win a medal and Eric's chance to rest. Earlier Beth had placed seventh in the 1,500-meter and the 500-meter races and fifth in the 1,000-meter race. But in the 3,000-meter race, she skated to a bronze medal. "I'm very satisfied," she told the press. "I skated all the distances. I did the best I could, so I have to be satisfied."

Beth (*right*) joins Bjoers (*center*) and silver medal winner Sabine Becker of East Germany on the winners' stand.

Eric and Beth meet the press after Beth's first medal win and Eric's third. Eric's colorful stocking cap was knitted by his Norwegian girlfriend.

On the next day, Eric was ready to again try his best. In this fourth event, the 1,500-meter race, Eric turned a near disaster into another win. As he skated through the first part of the race, he felt strong and ready to skate a fast race. But in the middle of a turn, Eric showed he was human. He slipped on his inside skate and stumbled.

A fall would probably have ruined Eric's chance for a medal, but he caught himself with his hand and bounced up quickly. Such a slip might have pushed most racers down a few spots in the final standings. But Eric was rocketing around the ice so fast the slip really did not matter. He was so far ahead he could have actually stumbled through half a lap and still won!

As in the 1,000-meter event, Eric won the 1,500 meter by nearly 1.5 seconds. Normally speedskating races at that distance are won by a few tenths of a second, so no one was surprised to hear Heiden's time of 1:55.44 was another Olympic record. Now only one barrier remained in the way of Eric winning five gold medals: the grueling 10,000-meter event.

United States goalie Jim Craig (*right*) stops the Russian team from scoring during the United States-Soviet hockey game.

The day before his last race, Eric decided it was time to watch someone else do the skating. The United States hockey team was playing against the heavily favored Soviet Union. It was the perfect event to get Heiden's mind off speedskating. Along with most people in the arena, Eric yelled himself hoarse. One of the American stars for whom he cheered was Mark Johnson. As he watched Mark, Eric must have thought back to his peewee league hockey days when he had played with Mark on the same offensive line.

The United States players celebrate their 4-3 victory over the Soviets.

At the conclusion of the final game against Finland, goalie Jim Craig stood alone on the ice, clutching the American flag and searching the audience for his father.

Two days after their Soviet win, members of the United States hockey team were jubilant as they received their gold medals after their 4-2 victory over the Finns.

When the United States hockey team rammed home a goal in the final period to win, Eric went as wild as the rest of the crowd. Here was a man who had won four Olympic gold medals in just over a week, and this was the first time anyone had seen him excited.

The 10,000-meter event, held on Saturday, February 23, was the race that worried Eric the most. It was an exhausting race of over six miles with a total of 48 turns. Since many skaters trained only for this race, most of Eric's competitors would be well-rested and eager to try their luck against the gold-suited wonder. Eric had not raced this distance very often in recent times, and he wasn't sure how much strength he had left. But the excitement of the hockey game had him fired up. Eric felt so good about the hockey team's amazing upset he could hardly wait to skate one more race.

Maybe because his hockey cheerleading had taken more out of him than he thought, Eric overslept on the morning of the race. Breakfast time had come and gone before Heiden finally woke up. He had no time for his usual three bowls of breakfast cereal. Instead he grabbed three pieces of bread before rushing over to the track.

A light snow had frozen on the track so many thought that the race would not be very fast. But when Tom Erik Oxholm, one of the first racers, got on the track, he blazed the distance in a spectacular time. His mark of 14:36.60 was just 1.5 seconds off the world record and almost 15 seconds better than the Olympic record.

Tom Erik Oxholm of Norway was the skater whose time Eric had to beat in the 10,000-meter event.

The scene at the Lake Placid ice rink seemed almost like a repeat of the 5,000. Once again it was Oxholm who showed Heiden that he would have to work hard for his victory. Oxholm's fast time bothered Eric. He did not think he could skate a world record after so many races. Yet to beat Oxholm, it would take something close to a world record.

Eric is closely followed by Viktor Leskin in the 10,000-meter
race.

In this race, too, Heiden was paired with another world record holder, Viktor Leskin of the Soviet Union. Eric skimmed over the ice at his usual clock-like pace. After only 5 laps of the 24-lap race, he started looking up at the lap cards. That meant that he was already tired, already thinking about how many laps he had left to go.

But Eric kept up his pace. Before long, Leskin began losing ground to Heiden. The distance between the two grew until Eric was 100 yards in the lead. Eric's legs could not carry him much farther, and he even had to stand up a little in the turns so that he would not stumble. But he was all alone as he turned the last corner and headed into the finish.

Normally there are very few people who come out into the cold winter weather to watch two men skate circles for 15 minutes. Even Heiden admits a race as long as the 10,000 meter is not much fun to watch. But the large crowd of Heiden fans at Lake Placid were enjoying this one. Especially when they saw Eric running away with the world record.

Heiden drove through the finish line with an incredible time of 14:28.13. For Eric it was the most satisfying race of all. He had smashed the world record by almost six seconds! The second-place finisher, Piet Kleine of the Netherlands, who had

After finishing his fifth record-breaking race, Eric is congrat-
ulated by Tom Oxholm, the winner of the bronze medal.

won the 10,000-meter race in 1976, was barely
within shouting distance of his time.

The fifth gold medal was Eric's. The lopsided,
runaway victory left no doubt that Eric Heiden was
the best speedskater of all time.

48

Eric waves to the fans who cheered his fifth gold medal win.

All the predictions about Heiden had come true. America had found its Olympic superhero. But all Eric had ever been interested in was skating for himself and doing the best job he could. When asked if he knew of any finer performance in the history of sports than his five gold medals, Eric had a quick answer. "Sure, the United States Hockey team has me beat."

Eric Heiden—the first person to win five individual Olympic gold medals

Though the 1980 Olympics are over, Eric will probably have a hard time returning to the quiet "skate for fun" life. He certainly won't be able to wander around Madison or step onto an ice rink without people noticing him. Eric is no longer an "unknown" star. Even the president of the United States invited Eric to come for a visit. As usual Eric said what was on his mind, even to the president. He urged President Carter to change his mind and let the United States athletes go to the summer games in Moscow.

Eric has said many times that he doesn't want to spend the rest of his life talking about his moment of Olympic glory. He wants to be known as something other than just a skater. He is not at all sure he wants to be well known. But Eric is certainly under pressure from people who would like to use him to help them make money. He has even been offered a hockey scholarship even though he hasn't played the sport for many years.

For the moment, Eric plans to go to Norway to study at a sports medicine institute. That decision is probably helped by the fact that his girlfriend, Cecilie, lives in Norway. After that he may consider following in his father's footsteps and becoming an orthopedic surgeon.

After the Olympic games, Eric and Beth are interviewed at a welcome-home party in Madison. A rally at the University of Wisconsin honoring them and other Olympic athletes from the area was attended by more than 22,000 fans.

It is possible that the sports world has not seen the last of Eric Heiden. He talks about taking up bicycling as a sport. Bicycle races are part of the summer Olympics games. Of course he says that he would do it "just for fun." But Eric was also speed-skating "just for fun" when he ended up with five gold medals!

In May 1980 Eric tried out for the United States Olympic cycling team. He finished second in the 1,000-meter trials and placed tenth overall, but only the top eight cyclists were chosen for the team.

ERIC HEIDEN'S RECORD-BREAKING TIMES

THE OLYMPIC SPEEDSKATING EVENTS	PREVIOUS OLYMPIC RECORD 1976	HEIDEN'S OLYMPIC RECORD 1980
500 Meter*	39.17	38.03
1,000 Meter**	1:19.32	1:15.44
1,500 Meter**	1:59.38	1:55.44
5,000 Meter**	7:24.48	7:02.29
10,000 Meter**	14:50.59	14:28.13

*time in seconds and hundredths of seconds
**time in minutes, seconds, and hundredths of seconds